ISBN No 978-1-84535-460-2

Dennis the Menace arrived in The Beano comic in March 1951. Drawn by artist David Law, the first strip was a black and white half page and Dennis wore a plain grey shirt and striped tie. This changed to a black and white striped jersey within six weeks and then in September, to his now iconic red and black hooped top, probably the most recognisable uniform in British comics. The addition of a mischievous grin and wild, unruly hair completed the style that had to live up to the billing 'The World's Wildest Boy' and in doing so created the first 'punk' look.

Dennis broke the mould ( and that wouldn't be all he'd break) from previous comic stories. He was the first anti-authority rebel to (dis)grace the pages of The Beano and The Dandy. His sole quest was to have as much fun as possible and pompous figures of authority and killjoy parents weren't going to stop him. The wilder the mischief Dennis got up to, the more the Beano readers loved him. Teachers and school authority were top targets for the spiky haired terror, creating a battleground that would be in action for decades.

There was no stopping the red and black striped menace and he soon took over the coveted full colour back page of The Beano . Dennis was on a roll and then chanced upon a stray Abyssinnian Wire-haired Tripehound in August, 1968. Impressed by the hound's granite-shattering teeth, Dennis called his new pal Gnasher. Like Ant and Dec or Morecambe and Wise, Dennis and Gnasher became a great comic duo. They elbowed Biffo the Bear from the front cover of The Beano and shortly after launched their own fan club - by 1988 it had a million members. Nothing stopped the terrible twosome and they went on to a puppet series then animated videos before landing their own animation TV series. In this, Dennis's 60th birthday year, the third series is on BBC TV and topping the ratings. Many things have changed in Dennis the Menace's 60 years. One thing has never changed - HE'S STILL THE WORLD'S WILDEST BOY!

# DENNIS the MENACE

CINEMA

WHAT A SMASHIN' PICTURE!

D'YOU SEE WHERE THE ENEMY AGENT SENT A LETTER BY PIGEON POST? **SMASHIN'!**

NEXT DAY

THAT'S FANTAIL JOHNSON'S PIGEON LOFT.

SQUAWK SCUFFLE

YEP—I'VE BEEN THINKIN'—PIGEONS ARE USED FOR CARRYING LETTERS—

—BUT NOBODY'S EVER THOUGHT OF PIGEONS CARRYING **PARCELS!**

OFF YOU GO HOME, MY BEAUTIES!

DENNIS'S PIJIN POST

IT'S LOOSE—IT'S FALLING!

**WHOOF**

DENNIS'S PIJIN POST

D-D-DAD!

COME HOME, MY LITTLE HOMING PIGEON—THERE'S A SLIPPER WAITING TO **MEET YOU!**

SKIRL SCREECH WAIL

HIGHLAND MENACE

CORKS

CRAFTY DENNIS

CORKING PLOT

FLYING SCOT

Dennis's "steam-roller" fairly makes folk holler.

# DENNIS the MENACE

# DENNIS the MENACE

# DENNIS the MENACE

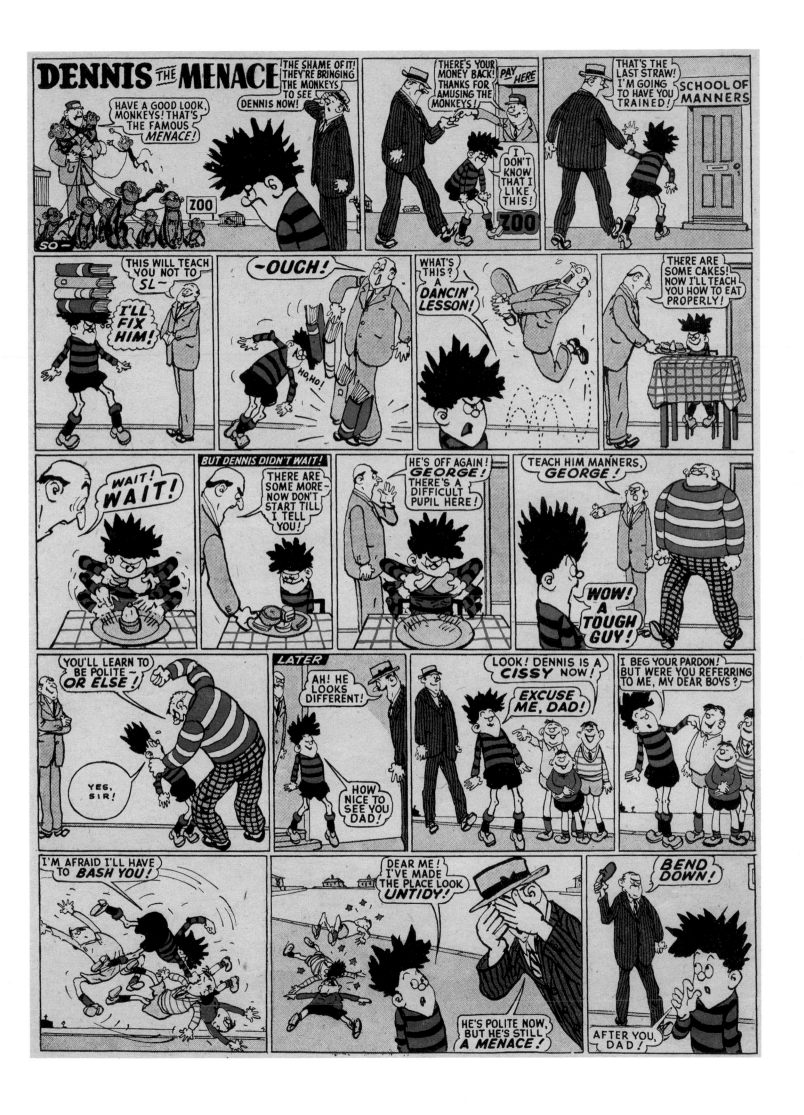

# DENNIS the MENACE

# DENNIS the MENACE

# DENNIS the MENACE

# DENNIS the MENACE

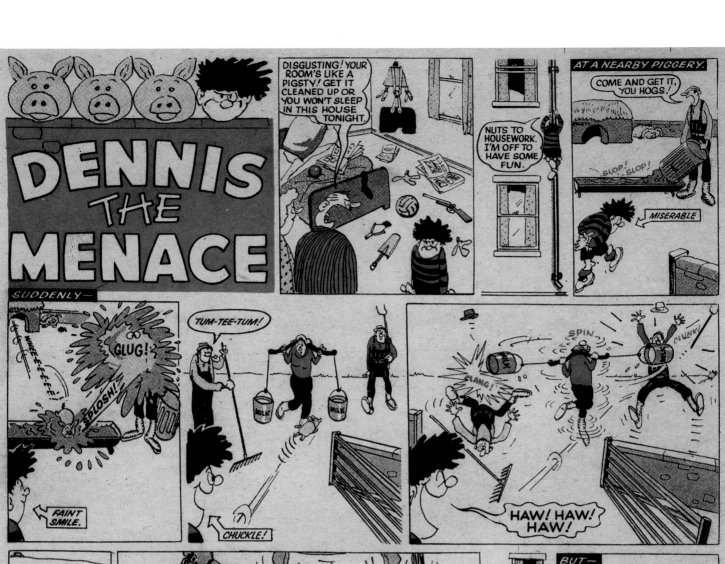

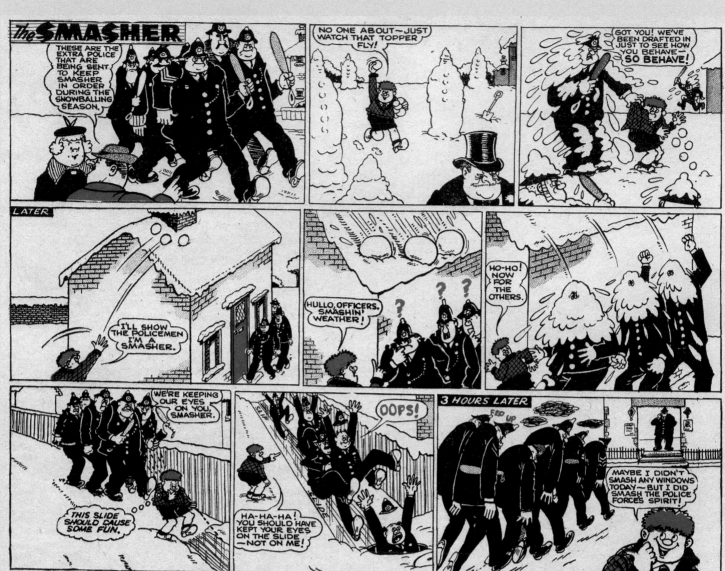

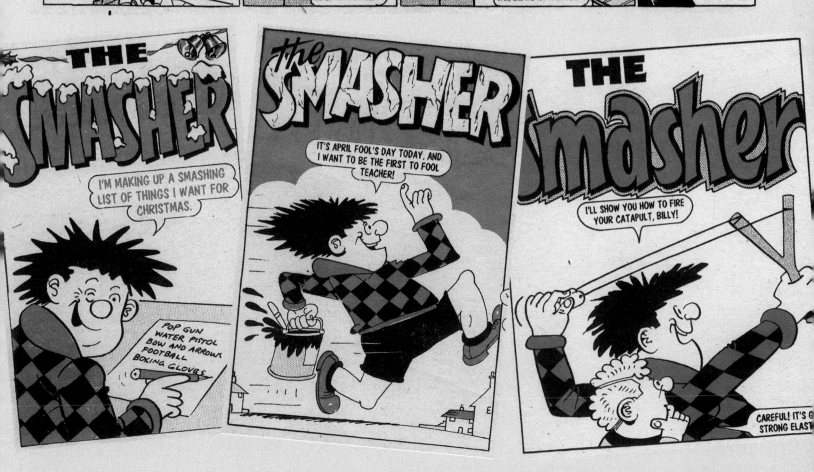

*Dan went to bed, and when he rose — He found he'd had a 3-day doze!*

When is a piece of wood like a king? — When it's made into a ruler.

In the fifties, Dennis did not only appear in The Beano, he had a separate weekly strip in the Weekly News newspaper. These strips were also drawn by David Law but did not appear in the weekly Beano. They were used in early Dennis the Menace books. In the mid fifties the combined sale of The Beano and The Weekly News was around three million copies a week so an awful lot of people were reading Dennis and his wild adventures.

Cover of the Dennis the Menace book 1956.

Dennis the Menace book 1958.

# DENNIS'S MODEL CAREER

Robert Harrop Designs started producing figurines based on the characters from The Beano and The Dandy comics back in 1994. Here he tells of his design work with Dennis the Menace. The First Dennis the Menace was sculpted by Matt Buckley in August 1994. The Dennis we chose was one drawn by David Sutherland in 1970. With Dennis the obvious lead character we launched an initial range of 12 figurines in 1995. The collection was a great success and there was an immediate call for a Christmas piece for the following year. In conjunction with The Beano we held a competition for the readers to create a Dennis and Gnasher Christmas design. Thousands of entries were received, the youngest entrant was 5 and the oldest 63. The winner was 9 year old Mark Simms from Hull and our studio worked faithfully from his winning sketch and so Santa's Little Helpers became the First Beano Christmas Figurine. This was so popular that it has since become a much anticipated tradition.

Over the last 15 years Dennis the Menace has featured in over 57 models, depicting the work of several different Beano artists. Two of the most notable pieces were the 2001 Red Nose Dennis, sold in conjunction with Comic Relief and the Lost Wax Bronze of Dennis 50th anniversary figure. This was a limited edition of 20 and literally sold out in minutes. We are currently producing the Six Ages of Dennis to celebrate his 60th anniversary, starting with the unique collar and striped tie drawings by the original artist David Law. This was superseded in just weeks by the iconic red and black hooped jersey we all know and love.

For your interest we have included photographs of the sculpting, casting and painting of the first 60th anniversary figure.

## Sculpting

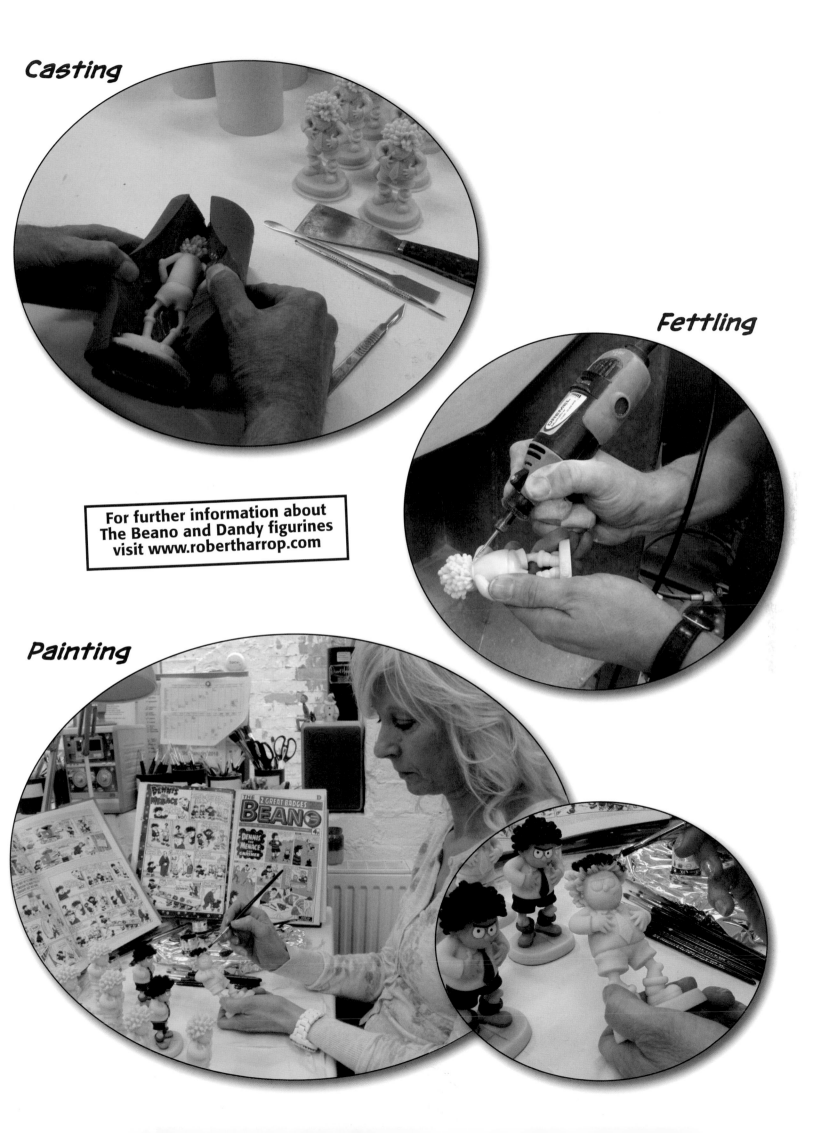

# Casting

# Fettling

# Painting

For further information about
The Beano and Dandy figurines
visit www.robertharrop.com

# DENNIS THE MENACE

# DENNIS the MENACE

# Dennis the Menace

WE'LL GO CAROL SINGING TO GET OURSELVES A CHRISTMAS TREAT.

HOW SPIFFING!

FIRST WE MUST GET SOME GOOD CAROL SINGERS.

I KNOW A CAROL SINGER WHO'S VERY GOOD.

LATER—

ALLOW ME TO PRESENT MISS CAROL SINGER!

UGH!

THIS'LL DO FOR A START.

SHRIEK! BAWL! HOWL! SCREECH!

INSIDE—

SHRIEK! BAWL! HOWL! FEAST OF STEPHEN!

GOOD GRACIOUS! THE NOISE WOKE ME UP IN TIME TO SAVE MY CAKE FROM BURNING!

SINGING SCENT

SO—

HERE YOU ARE, LITTLE ONES—AND PLEASE ACCEPT THIS SLICE OF CAKE.

TINKLE

OUTSIDE ANOTHER HOUSE —

LET'S GIVE OLD WENCESLAS BIG LICKS AGAIN! ONE, TWO, THREE—

INSIDE—

GOOD GRIEF! THAT STRAY DOG'S GOING TO SNAFFLE MY TURKEY AND I'M TOO FAR AWAY TO STOP IT!

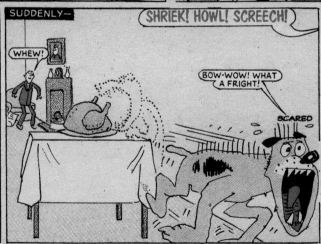

SUDDENLY—

SHRIEK! HOWL! SCREECH!

WHEW!

BOW-WOW! WHAT A FRIGHT!

SCARED

WELL DONE, CHILDREN! HAVE SOME TURKEY, TOO.

COO! TA, MISTER!

WHOOR—
SLURP!
CRUNCH!
YUM!
SQUEAK!

WHAT ARE THEY SINGING NOW?

HEH-HEH! WE'VE GIVEN UP SINGING—WE'RE SCOFFING THE TUCK NOW!

WE SAVED SOME FOR YOU—MERRY CHRISTMAS, READERS!

# DENNIS the MENACE

# ♫ DENNIS THE MENACE ♫

OF COURSE WALTER AND WINIFRED WILL WIN THE JUNIOR BALLROOM DANCING CONTEST. YOUR CLUMSY SON WOULDN'T HAVE A HOPE!

SHAME

WE'LL SEE ABOUT THAT!

GRIM

COUSIN DENISE IS STILL STAYING WITH THE FAMILY— I'VE ENTERED YOU IN A CONTEST AGAINST WALTER.

GOOD!

I HOPE IT'S A BOXING CONTEST!

NO! IT'S A BALLROOM DANCING CONTEST!

OH, NO!

LATER— YOU LOOK VERY NICE.

I FEEL A PROPER SOFTIE!

THE CONTEST BEGINS—

TA-RUM-PUM! PUM!

I LOVE DOING THE "MILITARY-TWO-STEP"!

GRACEFUL

DISGRACEFUL

EEK!

I LIKE THE HIGH-KICKING PART!

THUD!

NEXT, "THE QUICK STEP"—

OOPS! THERE GOES MY COLLECTION OF PET BEETLES!

WHIRL

SHRIEK!  WHIMPER!

GOING SO SOON?

AAGH! SAVE ME, DADDY! NASTY BEETLES!

SCREECH!

THEN— AS ALL THE OTHER DANCERS LEFT BEFORE THE CONTEST ENDED, THE WINNERS ARE COUPLE THIRTEEN!

PRIDE    SHAME

13

WALTER'S DAD

I'LL NEVER UNDERSTAND DADS! LAST WEEK WE WERE BAD AND GOT SIX OF THE BEST— THIS WEEK WE GOT HALF A CROWN!

This front and back cover from the Dennis the Menace book 1962 was one of the finest scenes ever drawn by David Law.

DENNIS THE MENACE

# Dennis the Menace and GNASHER

A Deadly Duo. Dennis teams up with his doggy pal Gnasher in 1968.

NEXT DAY –

TOSS

AUNT GERTRUDE'S PESKY PEKE, FANG KU'S STILL WITH US! WISH I WAS A BLACK BELT AT JUDO LIKE HIM!

LOOK AT THE SUPER WHITE SILK PYJAMAS MUMSIE BOUGHT ME!

WALTER THE SOFTIE

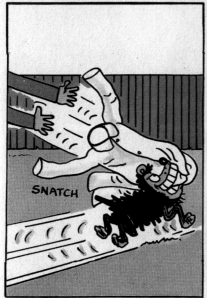

SNATCH

SOON– MAYBE I CAN BECOME A BLACK BELT AT JUDO IF I WEAR THE PROPER GEAR!

AND –

I'LL SNEAK UP FROM BEHIND!

GNERK!

GNEEK!

LIKE MY CELEBRATED NOSE THROW?

OH, DEAR! YOU'RE NOT JUST A BLACK BELT YOU'RE BLACK ALL OVER!

# FUNNIER THAN A HIPPO WITH HICCUPS

# THE DANDY

**55p**

Canada $2.50

DANDY Website www.dandy.com email dandy@dcthomson.co.uk   Every Saturday No. 3121 September 15th, 2001

# BULLY BEEF AND CHIPS

YOU LOOK VERY SMART, BULLY BEEF. YOU'RE SURE TO WIN A PRIZE AT THE FANCY DRESS PARTY.

I'D BETTER! IF ANYONE LAUGHS AT ME I'LL SLAY THEM!

HO-HO! WHAT ARE YOU SUPPOSED TO BE, BULLY MACBEEF?

GRR! I'LL SHOW YOU WHAT, YOU GRINNING BABOON!

JUST WATCH ME FLATTEN CHIPS BY THROWING THIS CABER AT HIM!

HEAVE!

WOW!

HEE-HEE! HE MISSED ME!

I SEE NOW WHAT YOU ARE—YOU'RE A FLOWER POT MAN!

GRR!

I'LL FILL MY SPORRAN WITH STONES AND FLATTEN CHIPS WITH IT.

THERE'S CHIPS JUST GOING INTO THE PARTY HOUSE. GOT YOU THIS TIME, LITTLE CHIEF RUNNING NOSE!

THE ROTTER! HE'S STILL AFTER ME!

TAKE THAT!

OOER!

OH, CRUMBS!

WHAT A SMASHING THROW THAT WAS, BEEFY!

I'M OFF!

NOW WE KNOW WHAT BEEFY'S SUPPOSED TO BE— THE FLYING SCOTSMAN!

AT THE PARTY—

HERE ARE THE PRIZES FOR THE WINNERS. WELL DONE, LADS!

MORGAN THE MIGHTY

BULLY BEEF THE INVISIBLE MAN

LAST OF THE MOHICAN

AND A SPECIAL PRIZE FOR BULLY BEEF. HE'S A VERY GOOD INVISIBLE MAN!

CHOCS

BULLY BEEF THE INVISIBLE MAN

THIS IS BULLY BEEF'S PRIZE. HE'S STILL INVISIBLE BECAUSE HE HASN'T SHOWN UP YET. BUT IF HE DOES WE'LL PRESENT HIM WITH A BOX OF INVISIBLE CHOCOLATES!

CHOCS

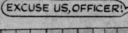
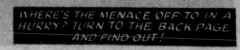

eano" Reader,
now a member
Club, and here's
mbership card to
Fill in the details
the card safely in the
allet.
r—always wear your
s.
All the best,
Dennis.

T-GNASH-YOWL-SNUFFLE!
nasher saying "Welcome to
Fang Club, too!")
club secrets overleaf!

is the Menace Fan Club."

STICK
PHOTO
OURSELF
ERE.

TOP
SECRET

ever Good!"
y Gnasher!"

S

by Fang Club Members.

SHTY!    Dinner's
         horrible.

big sister's always
ng on at me.

TTY—    I'm well-
        behaved.

well-
d.

NIGHT—    Sleep
          well.

## CLUB BADGES

There are many ways to wear your badges. Each position has a different meaning.

I read the "Beano" every week.

I need my dinner.

I'm top of my class.

I'm foot of my class.

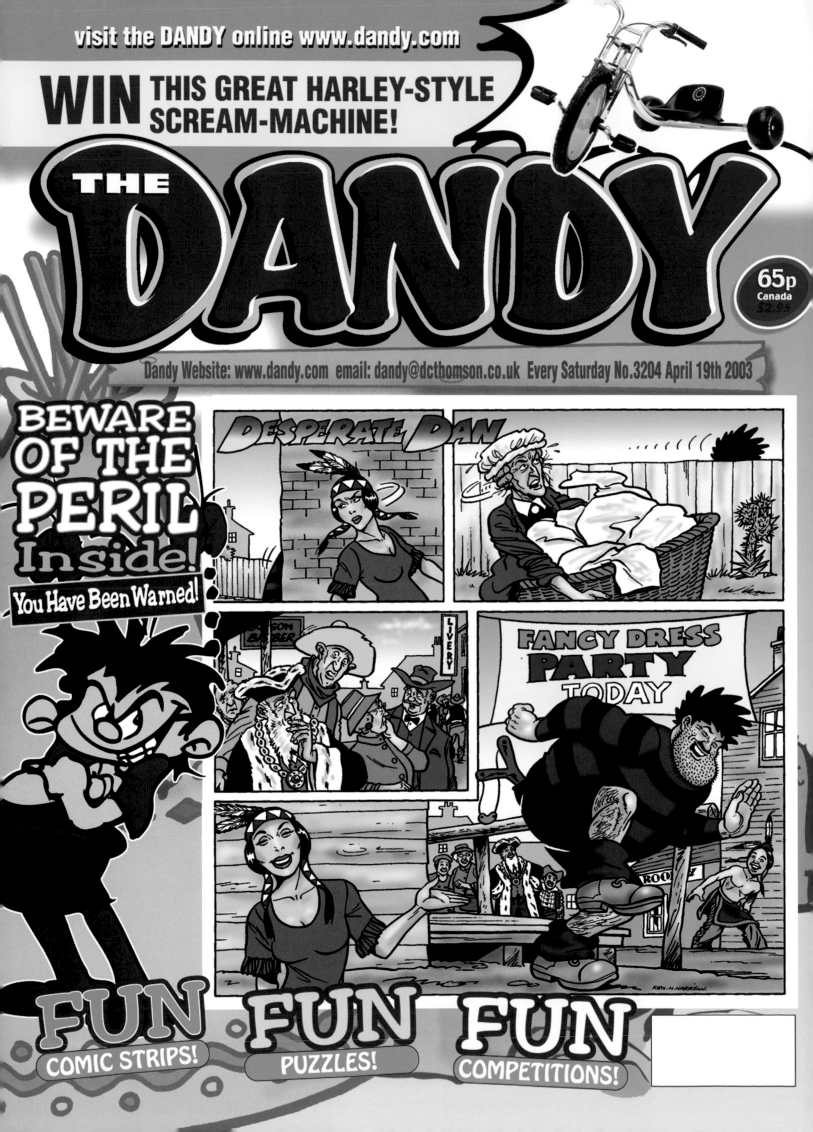

## Musical Chairs

This game is an old favourite with children. Set out a number of chairs in an area where there is plenty of space. (see fig 1.)

Fig 1. Musical Chairs

ALL RIGHT, EVERYONE, THIS IS HOW THE GAME IS PLAYED...

WHEN THE MUSIC STARTS, THE TEN OF YOU WALK AROUND THESE NINE CHAIRS...

...AND WHEN THE MUSIC STOPS, EACH ONE OF YOU TRIES TO SIT ON A CHAIR.

...THE ONE LEFT WITHOUT A CHAIR IS OUT OF THE GAME.

THEN WE TAKE AWAY A CHAIR AND REPEAT THE PROCESS UNTIL WE HAVE A WINNER!

DOES EVERYONE UNDERSTAND?

ER...

YES!

ALL RIGHT! LET THE GAME BEGIN!

CLICK!

...NELLIE THE ELEPHANT PACKED HER TRUNK AND SAID GOOD-BY

CLAP! CLAP! CLAP!

OFF SHE WENT WITH

AND LET'S STOP THE MUSIC ...NOW!

CLICK!

AAAH! OUCH! OOF! SHOVE! BARGE! BITE!

7

**Pass the Parcel**

This popular party game requires a fair amount of preparation.

AAAH! ... HAVE YOU GOT A SORE BOTTY, DENNIS..?

PFFF...!

I'LL GIVE YOU A SORE HEAD IF YOU DON'T...

ER... *COULD* YOU ALL PAY ATTENTION, PLEASE?!

ALL RIGHT, EVERYONE, PLEASE SIT 'ROUND IN A CIRCLE ...

When the music plays, the parcel is passed around the circle. When the music is stopped, the player that is the parcel must unwrap as much of parcel as he can before music begin.

NOW, WHEN THE MUSIC PLAYS, EVERYONE PASSES THE PARCEL AROUND THE CIRCLE...

... BUT WHEN THE MUSIC STOPS, THE PERSON WITH THE PARCEL MUST TRY TO OPEN IT AS FAST AS THEY CAN!

THE PLAYER WHO GETS TO UNWRAP THE PRIZE WINS IT!

ER... JUST STICKING IT BACK ON...!

RIGHT! LET'S START THE GAME!

CLICK!

JACK AND JILL WENT UP THE HILL TO FETCH A PAIL OF WATER...

THIS REALLY IS A BIT SOPPY, DENNIS!

YES, I KNOW...

JACK CAME... CLICK!

HEY, IT'S ME!

... THAT'S WHY I'VE BOOBY-TRAPPED THE PARCELS!

RiiiP!

SPLAT!

FLOUR

# DANDY DAYS in BEANOTOWN

Dandy Embassy

HEY! THERE'S A LOT OF RIVALRY BETWEEN THE DANDY AND BEANO RACE CARS.

KORKY 1

DODGER 1

2

VROOOM!

OF COURSE DENNIS THE MENACE AND MYSELF WON'T GET INVOLVED.

Wanna bet?

MY RACE BIKE IS FASTER THAN YOUR MENACE MACHINE, DENNIS.

RUBBISH! MY RACE CAR MAKES YOUR BIKE LOOK LIKE A RUPTURED SNAIL!

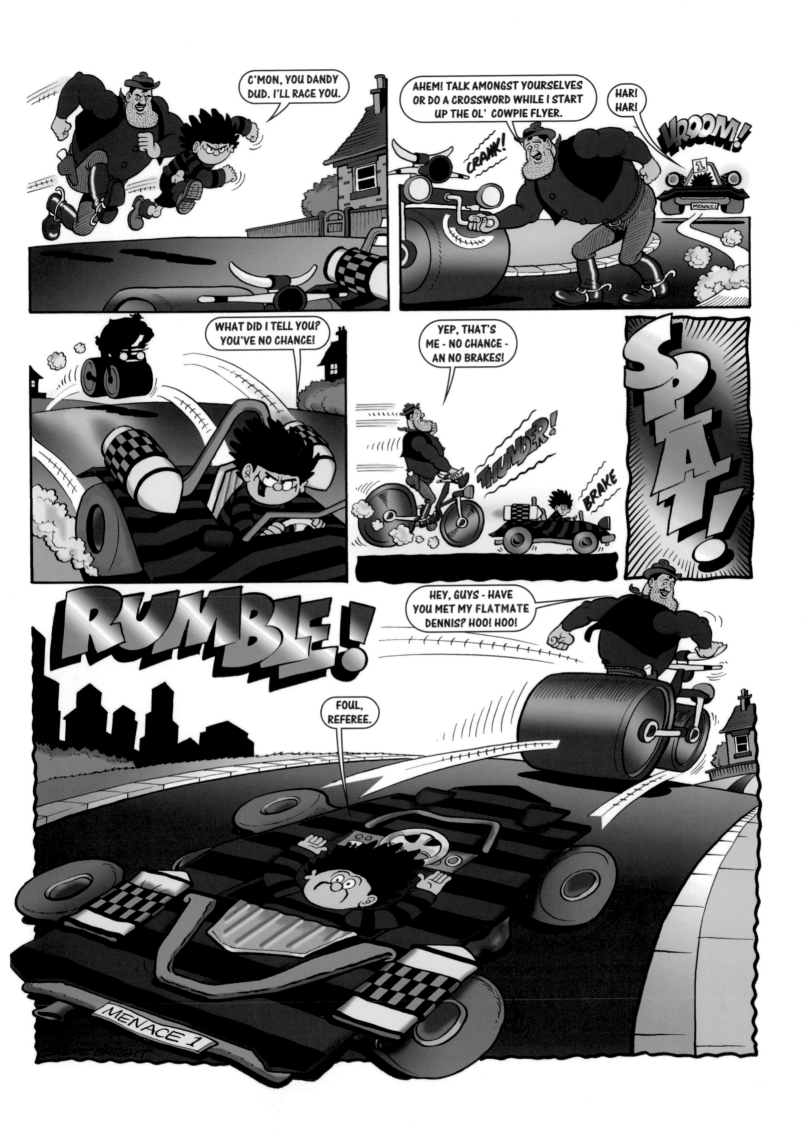

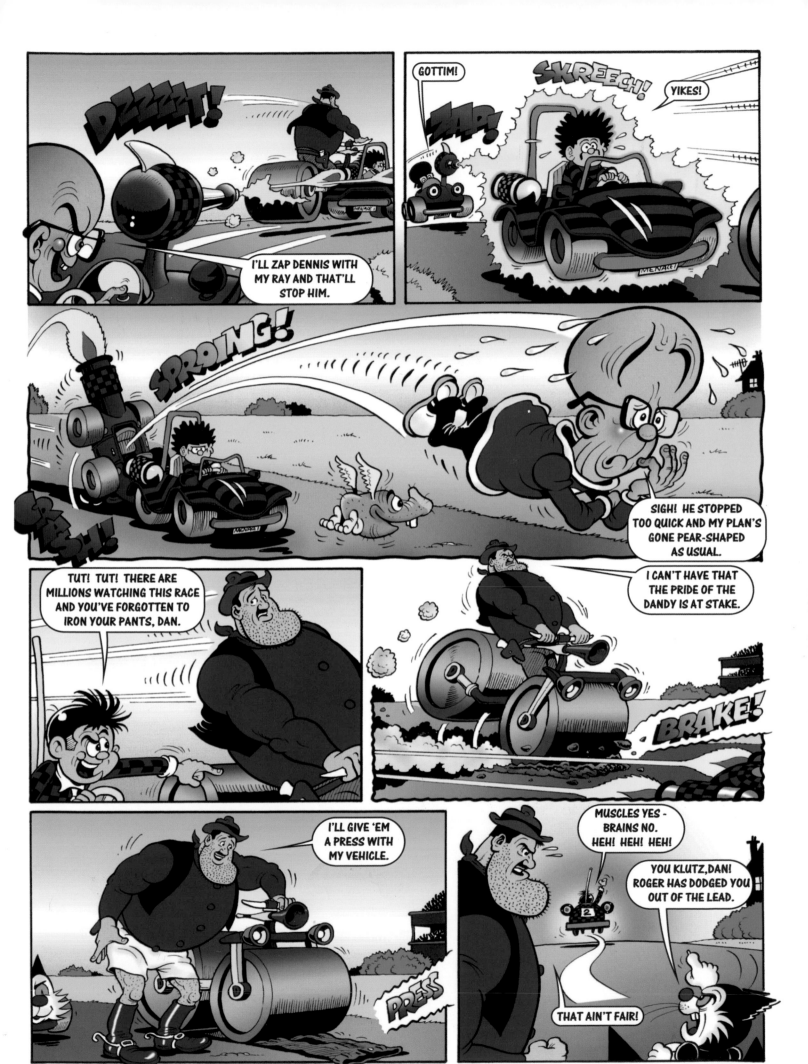

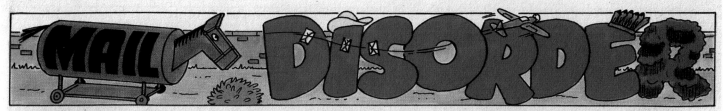

IT'S STUFFY IN HERE.

INHALE

HORRIBLE ODOUR

COMPOST HEAP

NASTY NIFF

RASHER, DENNIS' PET PORKER.

FAINT

PONG

THAT SMELLY PIG NEEDS CLEANED UP!

CAN'T LET HIM DO THAT TO POOR RASHER!

TURN ON THE TAP, MUM.

MUST SAVE MY PIGGY PAL!

CHOMP!

HAW-HAW-HAW!

SWOOSH!

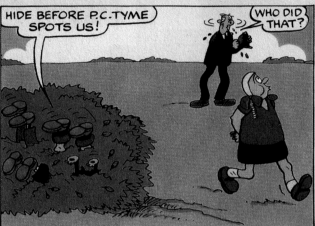

# Ok if I bring back a few friends?

For one week only, to celebrate **65** years of the UK's Number One Comic, Dennis has dusted off the cobwebs from some of the original team of stars from July 30th, 1938. Prepare for some fun as today's cast bring the "oldies" right up to date.

**< Ping The Elastic Man**
The only elastic man in the whole world. Ping often ended up tied in knots.

**< Big Eggo**
The original cover star, Eggo liked plenty of iron in his diet - kettles, old bikes, coal scuttles - the lot!

**Tom Thumb**
Only six inches high but he had **BIG** adventures.

**< Morgyn the Mighty**
A cross between Desperate Dan and Tarzan, Morgyn was cast away on a remote island for many years.

**Lord Snooty**
Lord Marmaduke of Bunkerton looked a real posh twerp, but he was a normal fun-loving kid at heart.

**<Whoopee Hank**
Crazy Wild West lawman who, funnily enough, usually got his man.

**Big Fat Joe**
Plump youth who enjoyed himself too much to go to Weight Watchers.

**Uncle Windbag**
Elderly relative of a young lad named Billy. Told tales so tall that they disappeared into the clouds.

**Tin Can Tommy**
Professor Lee and his wife wanted a son, so the Prof made them one out of old pieces of metal.

**Hooky's Magig Bowler Hat**
After an act of kindness to an Indian carpet seller, Little Hooky Higs was given a magic bowler hat containing a wish granting genie. This sort of thing happened every day back in 1938!

**Hairy Dan**
Old man - hairy face!

**Cracker Jack >**
The Wonder Whip-Man who could do all sorts of amazing tricks with a long strand of leather.

# DENNIS the MENACE and GNASHER

# THE BEANO BOOK 2001

## DENNIS THE MENACE IN ROBOT RUMBLE!

I'VE BEEN TUNING UP MY BRILLIANT MENACECAR.

WONDER IF OUR NEW TURBO-BOOST ENGINE WORKS?

ROAR! VOOM!

W-WOW! IT CERTAINLY DOES!

Back in Beanotown —

# Dennis and GNASHER

In 2009 a brand new Dennis and Gnasher animated TV series was launched.

Some fabulous design work was done for the series and we were introduced to some great new characters , including-

*MRS CREECHER* - Dennis's teacher, she's more than aware of the sort of scams Dennis gets up to and she's more than willing to hit him with detention. Which she does regularly.

*MR SCRIMP* - Dennis's Dad's boss. He's rude, greedy, bad-mannered and bad-tempered. He likes to shout at people, mainly Dennis's dad who he calls 'Whasssisname'.

*ATHENA* - She is in the same school class as Dennis but her dad is the rock mega star, Ratbucket, and her mum is a supermodel so Athena sees herself as an A-list celebrity. Dennis loves to prank this spoiled, rich girl and her pampered doggy, Miss Mini-Wuff.

Dennis's House and Tree-House.
The Tree-house is where Dennis and his gang go to hang out and play music, games and hatch their plots. It's their special place where all their most secret stuff is kept. There is a sideways lift between Dennis's bedroom and the Tree-house.

Inside the Tree-house.